Etiquette fc

(*E*4E)

A Technical Guide for STEM Professionals

By David Potts
With Kelly Harris

www.etiquetteforengineers.com

Etiquette for Engineers® is a registered trademark of Tazewell Strategies.

Published by Broken Column Press, LLC
BrokenColumnPress.com

Editor - Carl E. Weaver
Illustrations - Kelly Harris
Graphics - Leilani Dimeler
Cover - Heisey-Grove Design

Cataloging-in-Publication Data is on file with the Library of Congress.
Library of Congress Control Number: 2017952986
ISBN: 978-1-944616-14-4

A portion of the proceeds from the sale of this book will be contributed to STEM nonprofit organizations.

Table of Contents

Read Me First

There are hard rules behind the soft skills
Knowing etiquette logic helps you navigate your way

For many years, Kelly and I worked with aerospace engineers, scientists, and IT professionals. Despite our different backgrounds, we loved being with the STEM crowd because they were smart and saw the world differently than we did. We learned to respect their attention to detail and fact-based decision-making and loved all the cool things they created.

During this time, our beliefs in the important role protocol and etiquette play in representing our organization and building relationships with key customers were reinforced. We witnessed first-hand opportunities lost because of failure to follow these rules. And we saw that smoothly blending in during formal engagements raises anyone's professional profile and increases access to key decision makers.

While working together, Kelly and I taught two corporate-wide courses having protocol and etiquette components: Customer Relations and Doing Business Overseas. I modeled these components on the military attaché training I received during my Air Force career and Kelly provided the protocol and etiquette expertise. I figured if a warrior could be taught to be a diplomat, the same thing was possible for an engineer.

Sometimes it was hard going for our sessions because many aerospace engineers are no-nonsense types who are skeptical of the value of the "soft skills" stuff. In a world where rocket science is easy, those soft skills often make brilliant technical professionals uneasy. But the hard reality is that without balancing brilliance with better soft skills, chances at successfully achieving professional goals are diminished.

Engineers, scientists and IT professionals live in worlds of rules and predictability. They're successful because they master things that make things work. Protocol and etiquette also have rules and predictability. By understanding and recognizing certain key principles, anyone can figure out what the process is and what the next step is. There are order and logic to protocol and etiquette. Yes, a lot of it was developed over time and can seem odd, but so is the QWERTY keyboard. It was created to prevent certain combinations of keystrokes from jamming manual typewriters, but we still use it. It's now an imbedded tradition - just like some protocol and etiquette rules.

If you know the game and what it's about, it's easier to play. Knowledge reduces anxiety and lets you relax and enjoy the moment. So that's it.

Here's a protocol and etiquette guide for the technically adept and socially challenged who relate more to Steve Jobs than Emily Post. It's the same stuff reimagined.

Technical Notes:

_____

_____

_____

_____

_____

_____

_____

Start Here

You don't have to feel socially uncomfortable
Upgrade your life with a new etiquette operating
system

Life was moving along quietly and
predictably and then you received an invitation to a
formal reception and dinner. This wasn't a total
surprise for you've just published your brilliant
research and you and other grant finalists are being
gathered for a gala event to announce the winner.
Because you're smart and work hard, you have a
chance at winning the award. But more
importantly, this event could increase your income
with fellowships and promotions. You finally could
move out from your basement apartment and
launch yourself away from that old couch and
pizza-smeared game console into a fabulous new
life with cars and condos with balconies. Oh, think
about standing on that balcony with a glass of
expensive wine or craft beer in your hand and
watching a breathtakingly beautiful sunset!

There's just one problem with that vision.
It's clouded by your fear of not knowing how to
behave or what to do at formal receptions and
dinners. At events like these, you feel about as
comfortable as Han Solo walking into the creature
cantina on Mos Isly. For years, you've said it
doesn't matter what you wear or say or how you act

and eat - it's how smart you are. The rest is for show. But you've secretly envied people as polished as Captain Picard and now it does matter and you're not sure how to move forward.

Well, fear not. Read the following instructions and you'll be as cool and shifty as Dr. Who.

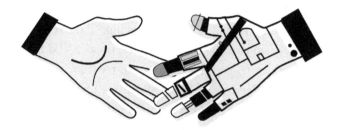

I. The Basics

It's best to begin with the basics. These appear throughout everything you do and with everyone you meet. Introductions, handshakes, and conversations are elemental and deserve a category all their own.

A. Introductions - *Who's Who?*

B. Handshakes - *Get a Grip*

C. Conversations - *Nothing Small about This Talk*

A. Introductions - *Who's Who?*

Observe the hierarchy of introductions
Make the effort to remember names

The proper way to introduce others isn't hard, but it can be difficult to remember. Usually, people make the mistake of saying, "I'd like to introduce you to" instead of the proper "I'd like to introduce to you," so don't even try that. Keep it simple. Persons of lesser status are always introduced to persons of higher status by addressing the person of higher status first: "Ms. (Higher Status) I would like to introduce Mr. (Lesser Status)." Then add something about the person of lesser status to make the introduction meaningful: "His work was recently published in *Scientific American*." In professional settings, gender and age are not considered. It's all about status and position. In business, the customer comes first. In informal social settings, it's whom you want to honor.

When introducing yourself, speak your first and last names clearly. Otherwise, no one will understand or remember what you said.

The hardest thing to do during introductions is to remember names. People are pleased when you've taken the effort to do this. LISTEN. Say it back to them as soon as you can (but not too often or you'll seem like that creepy car sales guy).

Try to associate the face with the name. Do they look like someone else you know with the same first name? Use a memory technique like "Dandy Dave Jones" or "Jubilant Judy Smith." If you can't remember it be honest and say, "I'm sorry but I can't recall your name" and repeat it back to them. This works once. If someone doesn't remember your name offer it right away.

In the U.S., we casually use first names from the start. In other cultures, remember to use the first name only after your colleague gives the okay. Until then, titles and last names are best.

Do follow precedence in introductions

Don't forget to add something of interest about them

Try This:

At a work reception, if Lieutenant Uhura wanted to meet her new boss, Commander Spock could say, "Captain Kirk, may I present, Lieutenant Uhura. Your new communications officer, she has a great proficiency in the nuances of Klingon."

In a social setting, if Lieutenant Uhura hosted a party and Captain Kirk wanted the introduction, Commander Spock could say, "Lieutenant Uhura, I'd like to introduce Captain Kirk. He, too, hails from Earth."

B. Handshakes - *Get a Grip*

A good handshake requires human input
Make a positive biomechanical contact

Legend has it that handshakes originated with warriors putting down their weapons, taking off their gloves and offering their bare hands in a sign of peace and friendship. This tradition is, of course, Western. The Eastern tradition is to bow. It's generally the same thing, but in almost all formal and business settings worldwide the handshake is an essential part of greeting new acquaintances and old friends.

Handshakes are the only time when we are expected to touch each other. Your handshake connects you to another living organism and transmits information. This can be good or bad. A good handshake, direct eye contact and a genuine smile can reinforce the positive image you began by confidently walking over in your smart-looking business attire and introducing yourself. But if you muff the handshake, it's like hitting your forehead with the ice cream cone. It's a mess and you can't really recover.

A good handshake is like a good space station docking. There are a deliberate approach and solid contact. Stand with shoulders squared to the other person. Extend your right hand straight up with thumb out. Make contact web-to-web between your thumb and first finger. Grip firmly (neither a bone crusher nor a limp fish). Pump twice using the elbow as a fulcrum. Then break off smoothly. That's all there is to it.

It's best to allow the woman to offer her hand first if she wishes, for traditional and cultural considerations. Avoid two-handed shakes unless you're running for office. Don't grab before hitting the web or it'll be awkward. And don't offer the power shake by presenting your hand as if you'd expect them to kiss your ring. If you're the unlucky recipient of a bad handshake, smile and take note of the personality information they unknowingly shared.

Do shake from your elbow, not your shoulder
Don't break off too late or too soon

Try This: Remember to SHAKE!

- S – Square off your shoulders, smile and make eye contact

- H – Hands should be dry

- A – Attitude. Make it positive

- K – Konnect (OK, Connect) web-to-web with matching pressure

- E – Engage with two pumps and pay attention to what their shake says

C. Conversations - *Nothing Small about This Talk*

*Ask questions, LISTEN, and take turns talking
Make conversations, not interrogations*

After you're introduced to someone, or confidently walked up and introduced yourself, you'll need to engage in conversation. If you were able to research the person you're talking with, you could bring up areas of mutual interest, such as why duck quacks don't echo. But if you don't know anything about the other person, try some Sherlock Holmes-style deductive reasoning. From their general appearances and body language, who are they? If they don't have a nametag with their organization you can simply ask them what they do. If they're wearing a special ring or pin, it's purposeful. Ask them about it. It's best to let them talk first and then you can comment on something that connects you, such as universities, parts of the country, international travel, sports, hobbies, whatever.

Remember that good conversations are shared and kept in balance. Someone who dominates the conversation might be interesting for a few moments, but you'll soon tire of having to be in receive only mode. At that point, pick a moment when the motormouth takes a breath, say how wonderful it was to meet them and that you're going to the buffet table (or bar). If they follow you, introduce them to someone else as soon as possible and keep moving.

Good conversations create new friends and make events pleasurable. Don't talk too much about yourself or criticize others. Find a subject the other person wants to talk about that you find interesting and stay with that for a while. Take turns speaking. People want to talk about what interests them, but many are poor at guiding conversations. Help them out by asking open-ended questions to keep things going. Occasionally you'll meet someone who's boring no matter how smart they are. Be polite and say it was nice talking with them and move away slowly, but purposefully. Life is short, so spend it where it's more fun.

Do be interesting AND interested

Don't talk too much about yourself

Try This:

- Closed Question (usually answered with a single word)
    - What do you do for a living?
    - Where did you go on vacation?
- Open-Ended Question (usually answered with a conversation!)
    - Tell me about your work.
    - I'd love to hear about that vacation.

Technical Notes:

_____

_____

_____

_____

_____

_____

_____

II. Before the Big Event

Now it's time for the fixin' to get ready to go phase.

    A. Invitations - *You Made the List!*

    B. What to Wear - *Orange is Out*

    C. Research - *Who Are Those Guys?*

A. Invitations - *You Made the List!*

Read the instructions and follow them
Don't surprise the hosts and lose your seat at the
table

Open the invitation. What does it say? It should give the essential bits of data for you to develop your plan: Who (the host), What (the event), Where (the location), Why (the purpose), How (you should dress) and When (the date and time). Use the invitation as a blueprint for constructing your next steps.

The first problem to be solved is how to respond. If the invitation is written it might have "R.s.v.p." and a telephone number or email address. R.sv.p. is French for "Reply if you please." Like so many things in protocol world, this has more specific gravity than it appears. It really means something like "We've gone to great trouble and expense to arrange a dinner with selected guests we want you to sit next to and if you don't confirm your attendance we'll think you're disrespectful and if you show up anyway we'll think you're rude (and an idiot)."

Sometimes you'll also see "Regrets only." That means you only tell them if you're not coming. Either way, a timely response is your first step in making a good impression. If it's an electronic invitation it's less formal but no less important for you to let your hosts know your intentions. If something comes up at the last minute and you can't attend, pull the invitation out of that pile on your worktable (aren't you glad you kept it?) and call your hosts immediately. Replies to invitations are like sonar pings. If you don't respond, you're not there.

Do read and save the invitation

Don't forget to respond appropriately

Try This: If you're the host, remember that people invite people. Companies and institutions do not invite anyone. If it's a professional gig, the name of your highest-ranking and attending executive should be in the "who" slot. Please note, that while the Associated Press style guide writes R.S.V.P., Protocol and Etiquette prefers R.s.v.p. to represent, "Respondez-vous s'il vous plait," which is a sentence.

Sample invitation:

Yoda

Master, Force Engineering

Jedi, LLC (who)

invites you and your guest to attend

a lightsaber demonstration and cocktail reception (what)

in celebration of Luke Skywalker's promotion (why)

June 7, 3 ABY

5:00 – 6:30 pm (when)

Millennium Falcon Auditorium (where)

R.s.v.p. C-3PO@jedi.net Business Attire (how)

B. What to Wear - *Orange is Out*

> *Business or casual? Match the impedance*
> *Neuroscience says first impressions are important*

The second problem to solve in preparation for the formal event is deciding what to wear. If the invitation says "black tie" it means a tuxedo with a black bow tie, in contrast to the very formal white tie and tails. If it says "business attire" it means a dark suit, not jeans and a black t-shirt. If it says "business casual" it means a jacket for the men with no tie. If it says "casual" it means nice slacks and a collared shirt. For ladies, it's generally the equivalent of these. There are a lot of variations to these rules and they seem to vary by organizations and geographic regions. So if you're not sure what to wear, get peer review on your plan.

Deciding what to wear before the day of the event can significantly reduce points of failure. For example, you discover hours before the event that the only clean pants and jacket you have are plaid. Two different kinds of plaid. Or your one white shirt in the closet has gone yellow. Or the only black belt you have was destroyed in that last unfortunate experiment. See - gasp - panic - collapse. Not good.

Your first impression is made visually by those you meet in the more primitive parts of their brains. This is the part that gives off the survival signals for us to freeze, fight or flee. In split seconds the brain makes a visual judgment. Friend or foe? Like us or not like us? Counter-intuitively, the key to success here is to stand out by not standing out. You want to engage the mirror neurons. Don't be the one who gets stared at for wearing the red bolo tie. Later, when you become rich and famous you can wear anything you want and be interesting. If you try it too soon, you'll only be eccentric. Like electrical circuits, you want to match the impedance.

Do dress to the expectations of the group

Don't avoid advice from others

Try This: Clothing should fit well – not too tight, too loose, too long nor too short. When in doubt, think classic quality over the latest trend. And the only thing that should be revealing is your wonderful personality.

C. Research - *Who Are Those Guys?*

Employ the scientific method and gather data
Prepare for conversations. It's all about them

Always research who'll be at the event before you go. This will serve two purposes. It'll make you less anxious about meeting other people and will give you something to start conversations. All good scientists, engineers, and IT professionals make preparations before they start experiments, designs and projects. The same should be true when encountering other people at social events. It's common to just show up and wing it. Approaching social events this way increases the odds of missteps and missed opportunities, but it's a variable you can easily mitigate by sitting back and running some web searches. For what purpose were you invited? Were there previous events of this kind? Does an organization sponsor it? What are its goals and who supports it? Who are the hosts? What are their backgrounds? Who are the likely guests?

Here's a little exercise that can help you get started. Say for example that you're going to a reception that Bill Nye the Science Guy might attend. Search the Internet for five minutes and write down three things about him you find interesting. If you meet him you won't stand there droid-looking but will have something to start a conversation. See how easy it is? Now do the same for some of the people you could possibly meet at the event.

It's been proven that in public speaking the more you know about your audience the more confident you are. The same holds true for social engagements. The more you know about the people you'll be spending time with, the easier it will be for you to approach them and have meaningful conversations. They'll be so flattered that you know about their breakthrough research in plasma physics that they might start talking on and on about it. Tips on how to ease away from a transmit-only discourse and other conversation skills are covered later.

> *Do spend a few minutes on the Internet prior to the event*

> *Don't focus just on professional interests. What do they like to do?*

Try This: Prepare three topics of conversation before going to an event. You'll always have something to say and never have to worry about awkward silences. Be curious and genuine – you never know what you'll learn!

III. Showing Up

It's time for the big event. You made it here. Now make it great.

A. Name Tags - *Who Am I?*

B. Receiving Lines - *The Line-Up*

C. Receptions - *The Big Bang*

D. Working the Room - *Orbital Mechanics*

A. Name Tags - *Who Am I?*

Badges help others identify you
But go ahead and introduce yourself

You've now successfully arrived at the event because you read all the pertinent information on the invitation. You're neither too early nor too late because you're considerate of your hosts. You're appropriately dressed for the occasion because you asked around and talked to someone who's been at a similar gathering. And you've done your research on people who might be there. Now it's time to meet and greet.

The first question: when should you wear a name tag? The answer is whenever one is provided. Although people usually wear name tags on their left side, especially men wearing suits, the proper place is on the right, below the shoulder. That way, when Juan shakes Susan's hand, her name tag will be right above her extended hand. She'll never know Juan forgot her name because she won't see him awkwardly looking over to her other shoulder.

Even if you've been given a name tag, you'll need to introduce yourself. Don't be that person who starts with "Hi there ... (awkward pause while leaning over to read the name tag) ... Bob. What brings you here?" If you can't read the tag or the other person didn't put it on, it's best to simply approach, look them in the eye, extend your hand and say "Hello. I'm (name) of (organization)."

> *Do place your name tag where others can see it*
>
> *Don't use only your nickname*

Try This: If you're the one providing name tags, remember what they aren't: a business card, advertisement / mini billboard, piece of art or an eye chart. A name tag is just that – a tag for a name. That name should be legible from six feet away in a clean, bold font. Titles, companies, etc. should be smaller... or not included and left for the conversation.

B. Receiving Lines - *The Line-Up*

> *Be patient and go with the flow*
> *Save your pitch for later*

Many large, formal receptions and dinners have receiving lines. These are not the lines for the reception. These are inside the main area after you've already stood in line to get in the door and checked in. Since there are lots of people at the event and usually only one host and one guest of honor, without this procedure there would be a rugby scrum to say hello. The receiving line is an organized process to quickly and efficiently get everyone acquainted with the key people.

A receiving line usually starts with an introducer, someone who controls the flow and gets your essential data to pass to the event host who will pass it to the guest of honor, all in turn. Walk up to the introducer, square your body, reach out with that great handshake and introduce yourself - full name and your organization. There may be a few words of welcome from the introducer and then you'll quickly move to the host. If the introducer does not pass your name and organization to the host, introduce yourself again. Thank them for the invitation and then move on to the guest of honor. Don't hold up the line by pitching your research proposal to the host or guest of honor. And don't waste their time giving all the gory details of the terrible flight you took to get there. If, however, someone else is being a bore by holding up the line, use the opportunity to be pleasant and engage in small talk with whomever you're in front of until it's time to move.

After you've been introduced to the guest of honor, and mentioned how marvelous chapter six of their new book is, move out of the line and enter the reception room. Some receiving lines have a multitude of hosts and guests of honor and even a person at the end who will direct you where to go next. Stay poised and keep smiling. The fun is about to begin.

Do give a good handshake and introduce yourself

Don't delay the line by talking too much

<u>Try this:</u> Should a cocktail reception be between you and the receiving line, leave your drink or hors d'oeuvres behind. Your hands need to be free for the handshake.

Avoid dumping the mixed nuts in your side pocket for a snack later. There will be food inside.

◀

C. Receptions - *The Big Bang*

> *Take a deep breath and introduce yourself*
> *Find someone interesting to talk with*

Many people view a reception as akin to being in a shark tank. You fear you're what's to be eaten, not an invited guest. A lot of this depends on what kind of personality you have. If you're more action-oriented and extroverted, receptions are like playgrounds. But if you're more task-oriented and reserved, as many engineers, scientists and IT professionals are, going to a reception where you may not know many people can produce anxiety. The key is to focus on a few people, pretend everyone else is not there, and start comfortable one-on-one conversations. You probably have more interesting things to talk about than that guy telling everyone how short the runways are at Aspen.

As with any other event, don't just show up. Think about someone who might be there that you want to talk with. What are three open-ended questions you'd like to ask them? The reason you want to consider open-ended questions is that you want to get them talking. That's the secret of success at receptions. Find someone interesting and talk with them. If you recognize someone of interest, approach confidently, introduce yourself, make a brief comment (not about the weather) and ask a question. If they're with a small group, join it if their body language gives you an opening, but don't barge in and blow up their conversation. Listen a minute. Many people are polite and will invite you to give your opinion. If not, move on and fish elsewhere.

Do come prepared to talk to people

Don't overload your food plate

___

Try This: Get a "wingman" to team up with for conversations. If you're an introvert with "nothing to add" but "misses nothing" or an extrovert with the "gift of gab" and "zero listening skills," teaming up with your opposite maximizes skills and comfort levels into a great conversationalist team. While one focuses on keeping an engaging conversation going, the other gathers information that makes the engagement valuable for the long term.

D. Working the Room - *Orbital Mechanics*

Move around and uncover new discoveries
Eat and drink like it's not your last meal

A great thing to do in a reception is to "work the room." Look around. Are others standing all by themselves looking even more uncomfortable than you? Approach them and start a conversation. Just because they're by themselves doesn't mean they don't have interesting things to say. If they really don't, you'll know soon enough and you can politely excuse yourself to go get another drink.

It's best to either eat or drink at any one time. It's too awkward to do both. If the bar is open, go there first. If the buffet table is lightly attended, go there first. At the buffet table, remember that it's not a food station at a refugee camp. You don't have to fill up your plate like you've just been rescued from a jungle expedition gone bad. Pick a few things that are easy to eat and ditch the plate as soon as you can because you'll want to have at least one free hand to greet the next interesting person.

Quite often a reception is an event unto itself and has more substantial food. Sometimes it's a prelude to a formal dinner. In either case, if you drink it's best to keep it in moderation. After that third gin and tonic, you may feel like you're the most charming person in the room. But your peers, superiors and potential supporters may feel otherwise. A reception isn't a keg party. It's a place of business.

> *Do talk with people other than those you already know*

> *Don't interrupt conversations. Ease into them*

Try This: Often enough you're not the only one looking for a social save at a reception. When you approach "Stan," he'll probably be grateful for the temporary reprieve from networking isolation.

Technical Notes:

_____

_____

_____

_____

_____

_____

_____

IV. Your Seat at the Table

The gong went off and it's time for dinner.

A. Dining - *Where Am I?*

B. Settings - *Table of Elements*

C. Continental Style - *Easier Than It Looks*

D. Silent Service Code - *Stealthy Signals*

E. Silverware - *Tools of the Trade*

F. Dining Tips - *Follow the Leader*

G. Eating Stuff - *Forks or Fingers?*

H. Drinking Stuff - *Wining Allowed*

I. Toasts - *Hear, Hear!*

A. Dining - *Where Am I?*

> *Find your table quickly*
> *Be at one with your chair*

The receiving line and reception are over and you're entering the formal dining area. Quite often there's a seating chart available or you're told at check-in what table you'll be sitting at. Go there and continue standing as others join you. Introduce yourself. If it's open seating, don't push a chair against the table, as that's dangerous to passersby. If it's seating with place tags, don't move them around to get yourself a better seat, as you'll incur the wrath of the host who had to balance the table with considerations unknown to you. For example, if you are sitting at the host's table, the guest of honor is normally to the host's right.

When the host indicates it's time to sit, pull your chair out with your left hand and enter it from the right. You'll also exit your seat to the right. The logic behind this rule is that formal dinners are crowded and everyone sitting down (and getting up) from the same direction makes for smooth landings (and takeoffs).

> *Do place your napkin in your lap after you sit down*
>
> *Don't put your elbows on the table*

Try This: When you don't know which seat to take, don't panic. If you're there to network, sit next to and get to know someone new. If you're the least "senior" person at the table, you have a couple of ways to go... sit next to the most senior and shine or sit on the far side and help the host shine by keeping the conversation going.

B. Settings - *Table of Elements*

> *Table settings have a particular order*
> *Napkins: Know when to hold 'em and fold 'em*

Take a look at the table. It's daunting at first, but imagine it's like a circuit board. Each piece has a place and a function. There's a plate before you. Sometimes it's the plate you'll eat off of and sometimes it's a charger, a placeholder or base plate for the soup about to be served. To the left is your bread plate. To the right are your water and wine glasses. An easy way to remember this arrangement is BMW: bread, meal, and wine. There could be a lot of cutlery around the main plate. Forks are to the left, knives and spoons to the right. You pick them up outside first and then work your way in as each course progresses. Fork and spoon above the plate? They're for dessert.

After you've been seated by the host, the first thing to do is pick up your napkin and place it in your lap. You'll use it during the meal to slightly dab your mouth so chicken grease won't be left on your glass. You can even stealthily remove that piece of spinach you know is between your teeth in your napkin, but avoid the urge to blow your nose into it. When you need to leave the table temporarily, place it on your seat so the wait staff will know you're coming back and will save your chocolate mousse. When the host indicates the meal is finished, place your napkin on the table.

Do keep your personal items off the table

Don't clean a stain at the table. Excuse yourself and go to the restroom

---

<u>Try This</u>: When opening your napkin, fold it in half lengthwise and place the crease at your waist. It should remain folded in half on your lap. When you need to dab or remove crumbs from your mouth, open up the napkin and use the far "inner" side of the cloth. This way all alien objects will stay on the inside of the folded napkin and off your clothes.

C. Continental Style - *Easier Than It Looks*

Eat more efficiently and effectively
Plus, it looks cool

When you pick up a knife and fork to eat, do you stab your prey with the fork in your left hand, saw it with the knife in your right hand and then put the knife on the edge of the plate where it slips off and soils the white tablecloth while you're awkwardly switching the fork to your right hand and go after that newly-cut piece? Yes? You're not alone. Most Americans do the same.

In much of the rest of the world, however, they eat in the Continental Style. Until mid-19th Century, most all of us ate the same way. Then some Englishmen, likely engineers, figured it was more efficient to keep the fork in the left hand and the knife in the right. Plus, it looked better. It looked so good even the French adopted this way of eating. But as with the decimal system, we Americans are still late to the party.

It's best to eat Continental Style when dining out if you can. It indicates you to be intelligent and refined and it's not that hard to do. Open your hands skyward. Place the knife and fork in your palms with the business ends resting on your index fingers. Grasp the utensils and turn them over. The tines of the fork in your left hand should be curving downward. Pierce the food with the tines of the fork and convey it (tines down) to your mouth with a smooth wrist and elbow motion. Use the knife to cut and push food onto the down-turned fork. Keep your forearms on the edge of the table and don't place your knife and fork on the plate until you need to do something else for a moment, like drink. Once you get the hang of it, you'll be surprised at how much easier Continental Style is than the American Style.

> *Do convey food to your mouth with the fork tines curving downward*

> *Don't put your knife in your mouth at any time*

Try This: Keeping your hands on the table, rather than in your lap, may seem like a pain (and cause a little). Historically, this practice demonstrated that you weren't hiding a weapon under the table. Nowadays, it means you are worldly, respectful and coolly relaxed.

D. Silent Service Code - *Stealthy Signals*

*Dine like a spy with a secret communication system
Help the wait staff know where you are in the
dinner*

Continental Style also comes with a silent service code. That's right, there are special ways you can arrange your silverware on your plate so that trained wait staff will know what you're doing without interrupting the conversation. For the rest position ("I'm not finished"), make an inverted "V" on the plate by placing the knife handle at 4 o'clock and its blade (facing you) at 10 o'clock. Then cross the tip of the knife with the fork (tines down) from the other side at 7 o'clock and 2 o'clock.

When you're finished, place the knife the same way as the rest position, but put the fork (again, tines down) alongside and just below the knife, with both handles at 4 o'clock and business ends at 10 o'clock. With the silent service code, you can keep eating without interruption and then have your plate cleared away as soon as possible. It's like an instrument reading for the wait staff.

*Do use the rest position when you want to pause or
drink*

*Don't converse with the wait staff unless it's an
emergency*

<u>Try This</u>:

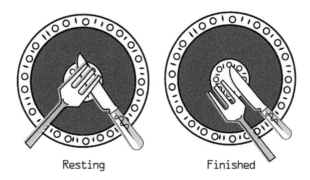

Resting   Finished

E. Silverware - *Tools of the Trade*

> *Each piece is a tool with a purpose*
> *Use them from outside in from soup to dessert*

Each piece of silverware is a special tool. Each is laid out according to its task and in the order that those tasks occur. For example, soup spoons. Avoid grabbing the spoon like a shovel and blowing on or slurping the soup like Uncle Carl. That's poor work with a fine instrument. Instead, grasp it lightly in your right hand like a pencil, but with the thumb turned up. Spoon away toward the far side of the bowl and sip from the side of the spoon nearest you. If it's the best lobster bisque you've ever tasted, you can tilt the bowl slightly away from yourself to get the last drop of it. When you're through, place the spoon in the bowl at the 10 and 4 o'clock position as before.

The salad is eaten with the knife and fork on the outside of the lineup. If you wish, you can eat the salad with just the fork, leaving the knife in place. When you are through, place both the salad knife and fork on the salad plate in - you guessed it - the 10 and 4 o'clock position.

The butter spreader is set on the bread plate to your left (BMW). That's your bread plate. Not the one on the right at a tight table. That's the other guy's bread plate. If the person on the left eats your bread, resist the temptation to call them out on it or snag the bread on your right. There will be more bread in your life. When eating the bread, pull a small piece off over the bread plate and then butter it on the plate before conveying it to your mouth. The person who pulls the bread into little pieces lines them up like bullets ready for battle is well-prepared, but not well-received.

Sometimes the dessert spoon and fork arrive with the dessert. If so, remove them from the plate and place the spoon to the right and the fork to the left (forks always go on the left). Sometimes they are set at the top of the dinner plate. In that case, when it's time for dessert, simply draw them from their horizontal positions down to the spoon on the right and the fork on the left. This time, instead of eating with the fork and pushing food with the knife during the main course, eat with the spoon and use the fork for holding the dessert in place and pushing. When finished, place the two in the usual position with the spoon up and the fork down.

Do wait patiently until your soup cools

Don't saw with your knife. Draw it toward you

Try This: If the soup is a broth, you may see a pointed spoon like a teaspoon. Sip it from the end, not the side.

F. Dining Tips - *Follow the Leader*

Be pleasant and know when to come and go
Look to the host's lead on what to do

The key to great dining behavior is awareness - of yourself and your host. If you sit silently in discomfort or talk nervously, you won't have a good time and neither will your dinner companions. Introduce yourself to the people next to you if you've not already done that while getting ready to sit down. Engage them in pleasant small talk until you find something of interest you both share, like quantum physics, and then ask them some questions about it. During the meal, do your best to talk with the people on both sides of you and even adjacent to you if the table's not too large.

So you've been sitting for a while. You didn't have a chance to visit the washroom prior to dinner and now it's difficult to concentrate. Or maybe you received a phone or text message (your cell phone was on silent mode, right?) and you need to go out in the hallway to talk. When is the right time to leave? It would seem appropriate between courses, but that likely will force your tablemates to wait to start until you return. Or you may confuse the wait staff and miss being served your filet mignon. A better time would be when you've just been served and you can scoot out before the butter fully melts on your baked potato.

In all dining situations, take cues from your host or someone at your table who looks like they know what they're doing. If they're doing something, like beginning their soup, mimic it. And if they're not doing something, think twice about starting to do that. It's like following the director of a project. Do what they do and your results will improve.

> *Do place your napkin on your seat if you will return*

> *Don't place your napkin on the table until you're finished*

<u>Try This:</u> Switch conversational partners to the left and to the right roughly every ten minutes. You'll soon see that if someone doesn't show, the empty seat makes the table dance hard. Always make sure to tell your hosts, even at the 11th hour, if you can't make it. They can rearrange the table and no one will be the wiser.

G. Eating Stuff - *Forks or Fingers?*

> *Baseline the taste before adding seasoning*
> *There are some things you can eat with your fingers*

You may want a little seasoning with your meal. If it is fine dining, it's prepared exactly the way the chef wants it, so no salt and pepper are needed. But if you're at a formal dinner with the multitudes, maybe your chicken a la rue needs a little help. Salt and pepper are passed together, even if you can't stand pepper. And it's best to try your food before you add seasoning so you can baseline the taste.

You already know how to eat Continental Style. Here are a number of food items you should use silverware instead of fingers in more formal settings: asparagus, avocados, cake, chicken, French fries, and fruit. You can generally use your fingers if the portions of something are small and everyone else is eating that way. Use fingers for artichokes, celery, corn on the cob, crisp bacon, hard-boiled eggs, shrimp with tails and small sandwiches.

If your fish is soft and boneless, only use the fish fork in the right hand (if you're right-handed). If the fish is not filleted or if it's lobster, ask for the vegetarian option as that's too much trouble unless you've done it before. If you get a bone, remove it with two fingers (you washed your hands, right?) and place it on the edge of your

41

plate. Lemon goes well with fish. Squeeze it with one hand while shielding it with the other so as not to spray your neighbor.

> *Do try the food that's served or stir it up if it doesn't appeal to you*

> *Don't talk until your mouth is empty. Small bites are better*

___

Try This: Remember to pass items to the right first (except port wine which goes to the left) before serving yourself. If the item never makes it back, you will have it again in your lifetime. Try and enjoy the moment.

H. Drinking Stuff - *Wining Allowed*

Water and wine glasses have different shapes
Red or white or both?

Your drinks are on the right of your plate (BMW). Say you need a drink of water. Before drinking, stop eating and take a moment to wipe your mouth so as not to create a food collage on the rim of the glass. Grasp your water goblet toward the bottom and bring it toward your mouth. It's best to look into your glass (never know what could be in there) and tilt your head back. This looks better than tilting your glass up and you'll get a better flow rate. It's not cool to drain your entire glass at one time like you did at that kegger.

There could be several kinds of wine glasses arrayed at a formal dinner setting. Sometimes they are in preparation for course pairings. For example, a Cotes-du-Rhone pairs well with your Duck a l'Orange. Or sometimes red and white wine glasses are placed depending on the diner's preference. Red wine glasses are taller and have larger bowls to accommodate stronger aromas and flavors than white wine. The water goblet looks different from both red and white wine glasses as it's thicker and has a wide mouth.

The rule used to be that red wine was served with red meat and white wine with fish, but there are so many varieties available now that it's like gold and silver jewelry. You can mix and match according to your taste. If you aren't sure, watch what the host is drinking and you can't go wrong.

One final comment on drinking. Where there are multiple wine servings, you don't have to drain every glass to show your appreciation (or thirst). Don't be that person.

Do try the wines recommended for the courses

Don't turn your coffee cup over. Hold your hand over the cup or any glass if you don't want any

Try This: When drinking wine, hold the stem, not the glass. And don't be surprised if your server whisks that half full glass of wine away with the course change – it was paired with that course and not the next. More is likely on the way.

I. Toasts - *Hear, Hear!*

> *Be ready to respond appropriately to toasts*
> *Be prepared to give a toast if you're honored*

Now that you've learned to drink artfully, you need to be prepared for toasts. In such cases, there may be a champagne flute at your place in addition to the wine and water glasses. Toasts are made in honor of someone or a special event. They can be prior to the meal or at the beginning of dessert. If it's prior to the meal it's usually the host welcoming everyone. Assuming you've been watching others, you haven't taken a sip of wine until the host does so or makes a toast.

It's traditional that the host proposes a toast to the guest of honor just as the dessert is served. If you are the guest of honor, you should remain seated and not drink in honor of yourself. After the toast, you should rise and respond appropriately with a toast of your own. This time you can drink. Your toast should be brief and polite, not rambling and rude like your Cousin Al at the wedding reception you're still trying to forget.

It used to be that it was bad form not to propose or respond to a toast without wine or champagne. It also was considered bad form to toast with water. These are no longer true. It's the words in your toast, not the contents in your glass that are most important.

Do save some wine for the toasts

Don't pile on unless the host asks you to make a toast

<u>Try This</u>:

- Rise and request your guest's attention

  "May I have your attention please…?" (No glass tapping!)

- Propose the toast

  "Please join me in a toast to…" (Focus on the guest/host, be brief and polite.)

- Call to action

  "Please raise your glass to…" (Wait until the end. If you say this straight out, they have to hold the glass for your entire toast)

V. And Don't Forget

Sometimes the little things make the biggest difference.

A. Gifts - *Give It Some Thought*

B. Thank You Notes - *Mom Was Right*

A. Gifts - *Give it Some Thought*

> *Giving - Make it memorable*
> *Getting - Be forgiving*

Perhaps you want to show your appreciation to your host or to a potential business partner. The gift doesn't have to be big or expensive, but it should be appropriate. Like the toast, the gift itself is not as important as the thought behind it. To make the gift appropriate and thoughtful, you might want to think about it beforehand and not just pick up something at the airport gift shop on the way to the event. Perhaps you learned something about that person's professional, technical or personal interests while you were researching them. What would create a smile when they open the package? What would they be pleased to display or use?

If you are a guest of honor and receive a gift, don't open it up and frown like you did when your parents gave you a pogo stick for Christmas instead of an air rifle. And don't put it away without acknowledging or even looking at it. Give a big smile and act as though that simple gift was what you've been wanting all your life, even if it was a green bamboo pencil holder.

> *Do be gracious and thankful if receiving*
> *Don't make it a large gift if anyone's traveling*

<u>Try This</u>: If you're completely in the dark about the recipient, something from your hometown might just bring a smile, especially if there's a meaningful story to make the gift extra special. Remember, a gift should be more about them than you.

B. Thank You Notes - *Mom Was Right*

Written notes give the best impressions
Electronic notes should be sent the next day

After the event, it's very proper to send a note of thanks. A handwritten note on a simple card is most appreciated and makes a positive impression. Think of it from the host's point of view. It's difficult to put together an event large or small. If it's a big reception or dinner, you may not get a chance to thank them at the end of the evening. The next day all you have to do is be thoughtful enough to write a short note and pop it in the mail (You have some tasteful note cards on hand, right?). By-the-way, this also subsidizes the postal service and contributes to the economy.

Strictly speaking, traditional etiquette rules frown on email thank you notes. These rules are easing, however. If you do send an email thank you note, do it the next day and keep it brief. You can mention future collaboration, but don't include a proposal and spreadsheets unless the host requested them. Otherwise, you step on your message of thanks. It's still not cool to send a text or to give a shout out on Twitter.

Do include heartfelt thanks for being included

Don't make it more than just a nice note

<u>Try This</u>: How many emails do you receive in a day? How many thoughtful, handwritten notes? Which do you think would be more meaningful and memorable?

Technical Notes:

_____

_____

_____

_____

_____

_____

_____

VI. Down to Business

But wait, there's more. Even if you didn't get invited to the big dance, you'll need to know how to do all this if you want to build your business reputation.

   A. Being the Host - *Adjust the Controls*

   B. Office Calls - *Visiting Their Place*

   C. Initial Conversations - *Hi There!*

   D. Business Cards - *Play Your Cards Right*

A. Being the Host - *Adjust the Controls*

Prepare the restaurant beforehand
Help your guests feel comfortable

As your prospects improve, you may find yourself needing to host a business meal in a restaurant. A great meal with a potential sponsor or client can increase or decrease your chances of success. Since you need to be in control of your guest's experience, it's important that you know the restaurant. If it's a new place, visit it beforehand to see where there are good tables for conversation. Check the menu so you can tell your guest what's served there and find out if it's a good match.

Most business meals are lunches, but breakfasts and dinners can also be good if you both have busy schedules. Make the invitation call yourself and explain the agenda for the business meal so your guest can come prepared. As you are inviting, they will know you will pay the bill. Make the reservation in your name and give full directions, including any transportation and parking tips. You want the experience to be positive, so reduce any confusion. As an example, is it the Army Navy Club in downtown Washington, DC or the Army Navy Country Club across the river in Arlington, Virginia?

The day before the business meal, confirm the reservation with the restaurant and call or email your guest to remind. On the day of the meal, arrive fifteen minutes early. Don't panic if your guest is a little late. If they have not responded that traffic is bad and they'll be there soon, wait fifteen minutes and call them. Don't start without them, even if you're hungry and thirsty.

When everyone is in place, offer drinks and spend a few minutes talking and relaxing before asking for menus. Indicate what you think are good servings in order to give your guests an idea of your hospitality budget. Match your guests in your own ordering. During the meal, be polite with the server and make sure everyone is satisfied with their meal.

After discussing the business subjects, you can continue with dessert. If your guest orders dessert or coffee, do the same. Settle the bill quietly and quickly and then escort your guests out the door, thanking them for coming. Done right, a business meal can be a business maker.

Do consider your guest's preferences

Don't mistreat the server

Try This: If the restaurant lobby is confusing, consider including in the invitation where your guests can meet you inside the restaurant as well... under the painting of dogs playing cards or by the flamingo fountain.

B. Office Calls - *Visiting Their Place*

> *Don't just drop by. Set it up ahead*
> *Be polite to everyone you meet*

Perhaps you met a great contact at a formal event. They invited you to visit them in their office. This is a great opportunity for you to showcase your talents. Don't just drop by casually, as good impressions are only possible with good preparation. Make email or telephone contact first. Find out exactly where their office is and all the details (parking, floor, security requirements, etc.). Don't be that guy who comes late to the meeting all disheveled and disorganized. It's a cool style for a comedy movie, but you don't want to be in a comedy movie.

Arrive a little early, but not too early. The person you're meeting probably has a busy calendar and they only want to see you at the scheduled time. If there's a receptionist or executive assistant, be polite and professional and engage in small talk if they're not too swamped with work. Those people are trusted by whom you want to impress and their opinions count. Plus, if they like you, you'll have an easier time getting back in the door when you need to.

> *Do show up on time*
>
> *Don't ignore the people in the rest of the office*

<u>Try This</u>: If you've planned for that perfect arrival and the fates are against you, pull over and call. Let them know the burning truck on the American Legion Bridge has you stuck. Don't leave them hanging.

C. Initial Conversations - *Hi There!*

> *Observe the space-time continuum*
> *Notice the little things and take notes*

Practice your opening conversation. From the research you've completed, you already know a lot about what that person is interested in professionally and start with that. If you know that you both attended Case Western Reserve, save that for when the conversation gets more comfortable and personal. Don't creep the person out by mentioning all the Robot Fighting League videos on their Facebook page. Be a talker, not a stalker. There also might be an artifact in their office that you can relate to and mention. But be careful. If you start a conversation about the Turboencabulator model on the desk and can't carry your own weight in a discussion about it, you'll be revealed as a poser and your trust level will plummet to subterranean depths.

If the conversation is going well and the person you're talking with is going on and on (a good thing) you may want to ask, "How're we doing on time?" You don't want to overstay your welcome. Busy people can typically give you thirty minutes. Let them decide to extend the meeting if they want to. Don't trap them in their own offices. And if at the beginning they seem rushed and distracted (they really may be rushed and distracted), ask them if the meeting is still okay or if you should you come back at another time. They'll appreciate the offer no matter what their situation.

During the meeting, it's good to ask to take notes if the conversation is more than a just-get-to-know-you event. Always ask first. It shows respect and helps you organize your thoughts and their answers and puts more data into your long-term memory. If you're using a tablet or laptop, don't put it between you like a barrier. If you're using pen and paper, convert the main points within 24 hours (maximum for detail retention) and file them where you can find them again.

> *Do get them talking about what they want to talk about*
>
> *Don't overstay your welcome*

<u>Try This</u>: Before you leave or in your follow-up email, summarize the meeting in a few bullet points. It's best if you can do this face-to-face, as you can get agreement on the details. Whoever you've been speaking with might give you even more information and next steps can be agreed upon.

D. Business Cards - *Play Your Cards Right*

*The enduring low-tech memory gadgets
Make them look professional and carry them
always*

When you're in conversation with someone of interest you'll want to remember them and have them remember you so you can reconnect. A great way to do this is through business cards. In this age of electronic wizardry, it's surprising that something as simple as a paper card is still useful and interesting. Perhaps it's because we've seen card exchanges in so many movie scenes or because it's a 3D object we can share. Some cultures, especially in Asia, have ritual protocols for card exchanges. Regardless, it's better to have a card you can share than to write your name and contact information on a cocktail napkin.

It used to be that business cards were expensive and specially made at stationery shops. Not anymore. Great-looking cards can be designed and purchased on-line. If you're not artistically inclined, choose a template or have a friend help you with the graphics, fonts, and layouts. Don't get too geeky with the graphics, but try for a different look that exudes technical competence. Get a nice leather cardholder so you won't have to pull out a dingy, dog-eared card from your wallet or purse. And take it with you whenever you go. You never know when or where you might meet a quality contact.

The time to present a card is more toward the end of the conversation than the beginning. You don't want to appear like you're handing them out like discount coupons. If the person you're talking with is senior in status, as many of the people you most want to connect with are, it's best to let them offer a card first. If they don't, think of an article or some kind of information they may be interested in and suggest you'd like to send it to them and ask for their card. Follow-up remarkably fast.

When presenting the card, offer it with the print facing them so they can look at it as they reach to take it. As you take their card in return, scan it quickly (this will help you remember their name) and perhaps make a quick comment on some part of the information so you can continue talking. Don't put it into your pocket without at least a glance and don't write on it in their presence. In a day or two send them that article you offered or a note of how interesting it was to meet them. If you hit it off well, connect with them on LinkedIn (you have a well-groomed LinkedIn account, right?).

Do be the first to offer your card

Don't forget to bring enough cards for everyone

<u>Try This</u>: If you'll be working with international colleagues, have your business card translated into their language – and have it checked by a native speaker. Remember, translators help with the written word while interpreters the spoken word.

VII. Foreign Bodies

Engineering and the sciences are global. Depending on your work, there's a strong chance you may go abroad for a conference or work. Whether you meet international colleagues there or here, there are things you should consider from the following cultures you have a high percentage of encountering. For contrast, the United States is included. Information about additional countries can be found on our website at www.etiquetteforengineers.com

Here are the countries covered in this section:

A. Commonwealth of Australia

B. Federative Republic of Brazil

C. Canada

D. French Republic

E. Federal Republic of Germany

F. Republic of India

G. State of Israel

H. Japan

I. Republic of South Korea

J. Kingdom of Saudi Arabia

K. Republic of South Africa

L. United Arab Emirates

M. United Kingdom

N. United States

A. Commonwealth of Australia

Communication

- Business discussions can be blunt and to the point, but often flavored with humor
- If you are teased, you are expected to reply in kind and with good humor. Self-confidence gets respect; subservient attitudes do not
- Modesty and equality are valued. It is better to be seen as a "good bloke" or a "good mate" than overly self-important
- It is important not to appear self-promotional when presenting a proposal, as a hard sell can produce a negative effect

Meetings

- Punctuality is important, but meetings generally start with small talk before turning to important issues
- The business culture is more group-oriented than individual-oriented, which means it's important to gain every person's input before proceeding
- Organizations tend to be non-hierarchical and managers are not expected to see themselves as superior to their colleagues, just doing a different job
- Meetings can have a "post-planning" style with little initial preparation. Being over-prepared

with handouts may be seen as an attempt to limit useful discussion

- Negotiations proceed quickly and without overemphasis on details, but contracts are detailed and firm. Bargaining is not customary, though there can be a little give and take

Etiquette

- Handshakes and first names come quickly. Business cards are exchanged, but without formal ritual seen in Asian countries
- Business practices are more casual overall when compared to many other countries
- Getting the task done quickly and correctly is more important than protocol niceties
- Personal relationships are vital and connections are valued, but gift-giving is not a common practice
- If business suits are your armor, consider wearing lighter colored suits during the summer months (December – February)

B. Federative Republic of Brazil

Communication

- In order of importance in business, relationships occupy positions one, two and three in Brazil
- Many Brazilian business people speak English well, but you still should slow your rate of speech and keep the acronyms and US-specific cultural references to a minimum
- Brazilians use a lot of body language. Touching among friends is common. Try to stay comfortable while talking in close proximity and maintain strong eye contact
- In this business environment, what people say is seen as more important than what is written
- Emotion displayed in conversations is not necessarily anger or loss of control but could be enthusiastic interest
- Expect discussions to extend a long time and for you to be interrupted often
- It is vital to stay in touch with your contacts between projects to show long term commitment

Meetings

- Punctuality in Brazil is relative. Meetings can start late and be extended, so leave room in your schedule
- First meetings may be formal with orchestrated introductions and card exchanges, but most are informal and relaxed
- Business meetings are bookended by small talk
- Agendas are seen as similar to traffic signs: suggestions only
- Meeting delays and cancellations can come without prior warnings
- Avoid scheduling meetings during Carnival week and the July school holidays

Etiquette

- Brazilians are fashion conscious and appearance is highly regarded and noticed
- Dark, conservative business suits are best, and they should reflect your level of importance
- Use titles and surnames at first to address counterparts and then shift to first names when they do
- Business meals are more for relationship building than extensions of meeting agendas, so save business until after the coffee is served. Exchange cards and gifts at the end
- Always say yes to food and coffee being offered at any time

C. Canada

Communication

- Learn a little French - it's the other official language of Canada
- Be familiar with the metric system (it also will help in the rest of the world)
- Avoid stereotypes. Most Canadians are multicultural and live in urban areas
- Understand there are regional differences in Canada just as there are in the US. For example, Ontario and Quebec, Atlantic Canada and Western Canada
- Communications are direct and Canadians comments can usually be taken at face value

Meetings

- Be on time for appointments or call ahead if you're behind schedule
- Take time for small talk. Know hockey and don't makes jokes about it
- Meetings generally are formal with a restrained approach
- Canadians at meetings expect the right to be heard and listened to
- Decisions are not ordinarily made until all the facts are at hand, so preparation is very important

Etiquette

- Respect differences. Canadians (mostly) like Americans
- Be polite. Canadian business style is friendly and understated
- Nurtured private relationships are everything
- Dress is conservative and weather-aware
- Thank you notes are appreciated (and surprises aren't)

D. French Republic

Communication

- First impressions have even greater impact than in the U.S.
- Always address others as "Monsieur" or "Madame"
- Be prepared to talk about history and politics before business
- Include academic degrees and titles on business cards
- Organizations have strong vertical hierarchies and business communications are formal and impersonal

Meetings

- Punctuality for meetings is relaxed. Appointments are necessary, but arriving ten minutes late is not late. That said, be on time
- Handshakes are the norm but don't be surprised if the French stand close to you and even greet you with air kisses on both cheeks
- Meetings are conducted formally. Positions and proposals should be stated clearly and logically. Be prepared for detailed follow-on questions. Avoid high-pressure tactics to gain a quick decision
- Eye contact has more impact than smiling in how the meeting is going

Etiquette

- Punctuality for social events is more rigid than for business meetings
- Gift giving is not common. Better to host a great dinner to show appreciation
- If invited to one's home, bring flowers, chocolate or liquor (not wine)
- Tailored dark suits with white shirts are preferred
- Be respectful of the French preference to keep their professional and personal lives separate

E. Federal Republic of Germany

Communication

- People speak with each other at a formal distance
- Eye contact is direct and conveys interest and sincerity
- Germans often answer the phone with their last name
- Conversations have a few sentences of rapport and then get to the point
- Written communications are frequent, detailed and lengthy. Respond quickly

Meetings

- Even being a few minutes late to a meeting can be seen as an insult. Early is better
- Meetings are formal. Provide facts and examples as much as possible
- German business planning is detailed and thorough. They do not appreciate surprises. Decision making is slow and deliberate
- When a German business leader gives verbal agreement it is unlikely to be changed
- If a meeting went well, they may rap on the table with their knuckles

Etiquette

- A small bow or nod often goes with a handshake. Matching this is appreciated
- Gift giving is not the norm, except when invited to someone's home, when flowers are appropriate. If giving a business gift, make it practical
- Business dress is conservative, though one sometimes sees white socks
- As in the rest of Europe, July and August are vacation months and not good for scheduling visits
- Germans enjoy their quiet and privacy but are happy to talk when approached

F. Republic of India

Communication

- Interpersonal relations are foundational to good business and need to be developed over time
- Longer than usual small talk is the norm in all settings. Patience is admired
- Culturally, it is difficult for many Indians to directly disagree with you, so be wary of ready agreement
- Senior officials do not expect anyone to question their correctness in front of others
- Specific questions are more useful than open-ended questions in getting direct answers

Meetings

- Important meetings should be arranged in writing and confirmed by phone
- Greet first and give deference to the most senior leader, but recognize everyone
- Meetings can appear deceptively informal. It's best to relax and observe
- Schedules are fluid. Late starts and interruptions are common
- Meetings without senior decision makers are useful, but only for building relationships

Etiquette

- Greeting with "Namaste" (*Bowing to you*) is common, done with both hands together and a slight bow
- Opportunities to share meals with business partners are very important and should rarely be declined
- If you are given a garland of flowers, take it off in a few minutes and hold it in your hand to show humility
- Remember that Hindus do not eat beef and Muslims do not eat pork or drink alcohol
- Small, nicely wrapped gifts are appreciated

G. State of Israel

Communication

- Israelis have different perceptions of time, space and values from most Americans. These constitute the majority of business miscommunications, not technical misunderstandings
- Most Israelis speak at a much closer distance than Americans and there is more physical contact. Don't be surprised if an Israeli takes your hand in a genuine gesture of friendship
- Be prepared to move to a first name basis quickly. In conversations, expect to be interrupted. It's not intended as rudeness
- An Israeli can see being overly polite and respectful as artificial, phony and weak. Directness and honesty are valued
- When an Israeli says, "Call or stop by anytime," it is meant sincerely

Meetings

- Israelis operate openly across organizational hierarchies and do not attribute great significance to various types of internal authority
- The business pace can be a disquieting combination of "in-the-moment" urgency and slower, more deliberate final decision-making

- Business meetings can be more spontaneous and improvised as if a family was gathering. They can start 15-20 minutes late without concern
- Negotiations can be emotional and even argumentative, but opinions expressed aren't always expected to be agreed with. A handshake is good, but a detailed, written contract is essential

Etiquette

- The standard greeting is "Shalom" (or Hello)
- Israeli culture has been described as more "polychromic" (relationship-oriented) in contrast to Western "monochromic" (rule-oriented) culture, sometimes meaning Israel can be perceived as a small country with a large family
- The Jewish Holy Day, the Sabbath, begins at sunset on Friday and ends at sunset on Saturday, so their work week is different
- Business attire is more casual - think Silicon Valley
- Business cards (in English) may be exchanged at the end of a meeting

H. Japan

Communication

- A person's last name followed by "san" (meaning Mr. or Mrs.) is proper. It is better that you do not insist they call you by your first name
- Keep body language constrained - no dramatic facial expressions and do not talk with your hands or point things out with your fingers
- Prolonged eye contact, standing too close and physical touching are considered rude
- Japanese are comfortable with silence - do not feel you have to fill in all the conversation gaps
- Smiles can have double meanings - either joy or displeasure (discomfort)
- Japanese are reluctant to say no in many situations. They may respond to a question with a yes even though they mean no

Meetings

- Punctuality is important - allow about ten minutes of polite conversation before turning to the subject at hand
- The most senior employees are introduced first - then others in descending order
- Business cards are more important in Japan than almost anywhere else. Think ceremony

- Meetings often are more for building rapport and sharing information than making decisions
- An atmosphere of mutual sincerity, trustworthiness and compatibility help meetings go well

Etiquette

- Dark, conservative business suits are best. Wear shoes that are easy to remove (and good socks)
- Japanese business people will likely greet you with a handshake and a nod, rather than a bow
- When greeted with a bow, bow back as low as the one you receive - or lower if it is someone of very high status. Keep your eyes low, back straight and hands flat against your thighs
- Most business entertaining is done at restaurants and drinking is an important part of business culture and communication. Empty glasses and empty plates indicate you want more
- Gift giving is important, more especially the style in which the gift is given: not a surprise, wrapped appropriately, generally at the end of a first meeting. Avoid clocks and knives because they both represent the ending of relationships

I. Republic of South Korea

Communication

- Always show respect to senior people and strive to create harmonious relations
- Open disagreement is rare. Therefore, never take "yes" for an answer of commitment
- Because business relationships are so heavily influenced by friendships, be patient and avoid embarrassing your counterparts at all costs
- The first two Korean names are familial, the third is given. To be polite, address them by title and the first name (Mr. Lee)
- Avoid touching and direct eye contact (except among friends)

Meetings

- Punctuality is a sign of respect. So is waiting patiently in the outer office
- Do not expect much out of first meetings other than initial steps in building friendships
- As technical levels of meetings increase, have details available so no one will lose face for not knowing them
- It's a good idea to send some materials ahead of the meeting to help manage expectations
- Meetings are usually reserved. If they become emotional, it's best to take a pause

Etiquette

- Good business attire and good posture show honor and respect
- Try to balance out delegations according to rank, so everyone can have a counterpart
- Present and receive calling cards and gifts with both hands
- Small, appropriate and nicely wrapped gifts are very important in reinforcing relationships. Again, avoid clocks and knives
- Be prepared to follow meetings with meals, drinks and even Karaoke

J. Kingdom of Saudi Arabia

Communication

- First name usage is common, though politely prefixed with professional titles or "Mr." for businessmen. Government officials are referred to as "Excellency." Members of the royal family have various titles
- When a Saudi says something, the words may have different meanings. Be aware of body language, facial cues and eye contact to assess context
- Expect probing questions about your work position and personal questions about your income and family. These help place you within their hierarchy
- Calm, dignified and measured speaking is highly valued, but speaking volubly by a Saudi may be a positive sign of interest and engagement
- Flattery is welcomed and, when returned, should be taken graciously
- Strong eye contact is a signal of sincerity and honor

Meetings

- Face-to-face meetings are vitally important in building relationships

- Try if at all possible to go to the first meeting with one of your colleagues who is acquainted with the person you will be meeting
- Always arrive on time, but don't expect your Saudi business associates to be on time. If they aren't, don't take it personally
- Meetings tend not to be linear, structured or time constrained. They will involve extended "getting to know you" conversations and may include others with whom the principle is conversing on separate subjects
- When it is your turn to speak, reintroduce yourself if necessary and briefly speak of your organization. Wait to get to specific reasons for the meeting
- Meetings may be set up several weeks in advance, though not always. Sometimes you wait for a meeting after you've arrived in country
- Meetings can be interrupted by phone calls, e-mails, texts and prayers

Etiquette

- Mistakes in basic manners may be forgiven for newcomers the first time
- Try to always accept more tea, more food, and more dinners
- Business suits and ties are the norm and the jackets stay on. Saudis wear little jewelry.

- Do not show the soles of your feet during a meeting (i.e. crossing legs)
- Give and accept a business card with the right hand and treat it respectfully. Avoid doing much of anything with the left hand
- Handshakes are common between men, but let the Saudi initiate it and hold it until he releases it
- Gifts are appropriate, but should not be lavish
- Stay calm - Saudis speak at a closer distance, may take your hand in friendship and, as your business relationship becomes more personal, may even greet you with air-kisses

K. Republic of South Africa

Communications

- There are 11 official languages, but English is preferred for business
- South Africa has a constellation of cultures with different ones influential in different places
- The people of South Africa are very friendly to those who travel there for business or pleasure
- It's important to build as much rapport as possible before one travels to South Africa in order to make the best use of limited face-to-face time

Meetings

- Business meetings have a warm tone and are usually very accommodating
- Friendly affections are openly displayed with shaking hands and even slaps on the back
- The pace of business is relaxed, on so-called "Africa Time," but punctuality is still preferred and appreciated
- Sensitivity to the realities of post-Apartheid is very important, as well as compliance with the laws accompanying it which give greater opportunities to previously disadvantaged groups

- Vacations are taken at the height of summer – December through January

Etiquette

- English social etiquette still echoes in South Africa, such as afternoon tea
- Continental-style dining is common, except for traditional African feasts where eating with the right hand is commonplace
- Wild game meat is common and popular and it's polite to not leave much food on your plate
- Elders are usually treated with great respect and reverence
- Small gifts are commonly exchanged during important meetings and meals

L. United Arab Emirates

Communication

- Since 80% of the population are non-Emirati, you'll need to be flexible in your communication approaches
- Arabic is a language of hyperbole, so be prepared for lavish praise as incentives to build relationships
- Saying "no" is culturally impolite. You'll need patience and persistence to gain complete answers to some questions
- Emotional outbursts in discussions can be enthusiasm for your suggestions, not anger
- Use strong eye contact to display sincerity and trust and be prepared to stand close to one other
- Because relationships are so important to their culture, Emiratis prefer to do business person-to-person

Meetings

- Meetings can start up to an hour or so late, but it's best always to arrive on time
- Avoid scheduling more than two meetings in one day, as ending times and traffic are uncertain

- Meetings often appear unstructured and attended by others who seem to have nothing to do with it
- Begin with small talk to build relationships and don't rush your main points

Etiquette

- Pay respect to Islamic traditions, beliefs, and sensitivities, despite the seemingly Western business atmosphere
- It is helpful to have a trusted colleague introduce you to someone of importance
- Address Emirati counterparts by their titles and first names. Status is important
- Avoid showing the soles of your shoes by crossing your legs and always pass documents with your right hand
- Dress conservatively, but well. Appearance counts
- Being hosted at an expensive restaurant can either be a sign of progress or a kind farewell

M. United Kingdom

Communications

- The Brits, in most cases, are very polite and formal and do not become too familiar with someone they've only recently met
- They hesitate to say no directly but sometimes indicate yes by saying nothing
- This is the culture that invented sarcasm; it should not necessarily be mistaken for negativity
- Body language is fairly restrained: they may be excited about something, but appear reserved, and they may be really upset about something, but appear polite
- As there is a tendency to read more into words than other cultures, it's advised to be absolutely clear in messages to reduce misunderstanding

Meetings

- Time is valued. Short notice cancellations and delays are seen as bad form and quickly erode trust and credibility if repeated
- Business circles are smaller and more connected. Good relationships are vital
- Displays of enthusiasm and risk-taking should be tempered
- Meetings are more information sharing than brain-storming

- Decisions generally are made cautiously after consensus is reached

Etiquette

- Privacy is highly valued and Brits do not like to be embarrassed, so situations may become uncomfortably quiet and too polite for newcomers
- Business attire is classical conservative
- Gift giving is not usually part of business relations
- Remember that not everybody lives in London, is a Manchester United fan and knows the Queen

N. United States

Communication

- When Americans ask, "How are you?" they don't really expect an answer other than "Fine, how are you?"
- In business conversations, Americans place value on using first names and getting to the point
- Those not used to American business styles may see "direct' conversations as aggressive
- Modest statements about yourself can leave an impression of weakness or lack of initiative
- If you don't ask questions, Americans assume you understand completely

Meetings

- Be on time for meetings. If late, apologize and blame the traffic
- Americans see a link between time and money. Long meetings with vague agendas may not get the results you want
- Your American counterpart's enthusiasm for their way of doing things can be calmed with factual examples of other solutions
- Be prepared to give and receive formal presentations (including data charts), even if connected via video link

- The usual goal of any American business meeting, even the first, is to gain a signed contract

Etiquette

- Because many Americans have never traveled abroad, they may be unfamiliar with common international protocol practices
- Business dress codes are so variable that it's best to ask before every engagement
- Gift giving is not widely practiced. Many companies have strict policies against it
- Business meals occur early - 6 PM for dinner - and you may even be invited to a 7 AM breakfast. Expect ice in your water
- Cards are exchanged casually. Handshakes and smiles begin and end meetings. Avoid hugging

Technical Notes:

_____

_____

_____

_____

_____

_____

_____

VII. After Action Report

No important project ends without after action items. This book is designed to give you simple and understandable techniques for how to navigate through the more common challenges you'll face. As you continue your journey into the world of protocol and etiquette you'll discover there's a lot more that can be learned and put to use. Here's the classic AAR format with some suggestions:

A. Problem Issues & Needs For Improvement

- For the latest in protocol and etiquette information, visit our website at www.etiquetteforengineers.com There you'll find more tips and more links to sites helping you solve your protocol problems.

B. Measures to Counteract Problematic Elements

- Why not get training for your group from someone who has experience teaching protocol and etiquette to STEM professionals? Kelly Harris offers affordable and entertaining seminars built around formal dinners where you and your colleagues can learn hands-on while enjoying a good meal. For the next phase in building your group's success, David Potts offers customer relations workshops and international business seminars. Contact us through www.etiquetteforengineers.com

C. Lessons Learned

- In science and business you should either win or learn. The same is true for protocol and etiquette. There are a lot of missteps you can make even with knowing the valuable techniques in this book. And sometimes no matter how hard you try, things won't go right. Don't let that worry you. Even the professionals mess things up now and then. If you're faced with etiquette error, don't panic. Keep your cool and press on, vowing never to make that same misstep again. Continuous process improvement. In a short while you'll be the one offering protocol and etiquette advice.

Made in the USA
Middletown, DE
17 January 2022

58844243R00060